This Book Belongs To:

Complied ,Written & Created
by Dianne Keast
Edited by Kerry M. Zabel
Search on Amazon
to see my other works in the
Rabbit Lovers Gift Set

Perfectly Sane Publishing Copyright 2021

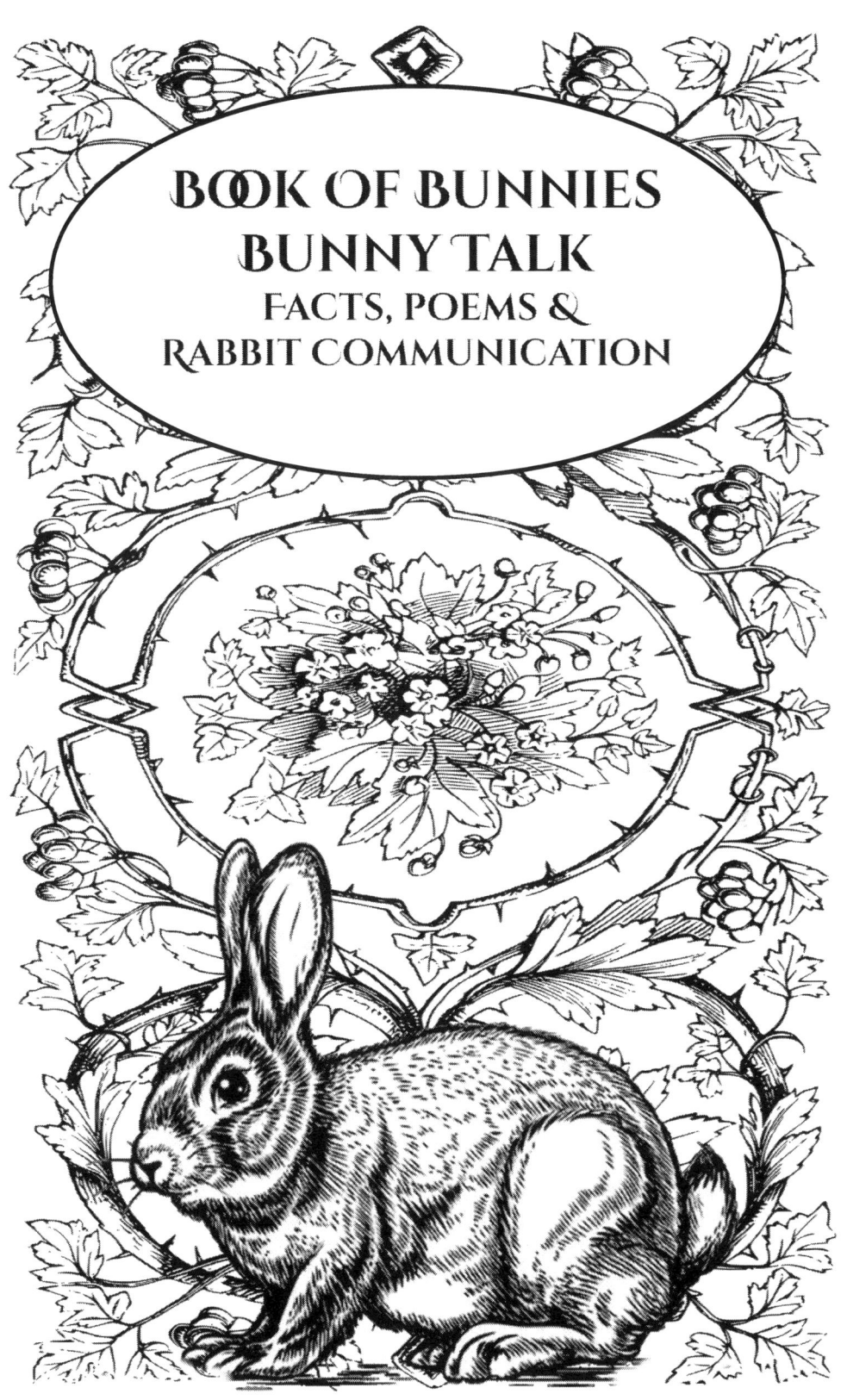

BOOK OF BUNNIES
BUNNY TALK
FACTS, POEMS & RABBIT COMMUNICATION

It's A Perfectly Sane Amount Of Bunnies! Thank You.

In Loving Memory of
Kerry M. Zabel
1971 - 2021

Our Fancy Rabbits.
Drawn for "The Boys' Own Paper" by F. A. Lydon.
1. Belgian Hare, 2. Himalayan, 3. Lop, 4. Flemish Giant, 5. Angora, 6. Black & Tan, 7. Silver Grey, 8. Dutch Grey & White, 9. Dutch Black & White.

About Bunny Rabbits and Hares

Once considered rodents, rabbits and hares have been discovered to have diverged separately and earlier than their rodent cousins, and have a number of traits rodents lack, such as two extra incisors in the upper jaw and differences in tooth enamel that cause rodent teeth to have an orange tint.

Rabbits and hares are small mammals in the family Leporidae, of the order Lagomorpha (along with the pika). Rabbits and hares were previously classified in the order Rodentia with mammals like rats, mice & beavers. In 1912, they were moved into a new order called Lagomorpha.

The genus Oryctolagus cuniculus, of which Lagomorphs are members, includes the European rabbit species, its descendants, and the world's 305 breeds of domestic rabbit; genus Sylvilagus includes 13 wild rabbit species, among them are the seven types of cottontail rabbit.

The European rabbit, which has now been introduced on every continent except Antarctica, is familiar throughout the world as a wild prey animal, domesticated livestock, and as a pet. Hares on the other hand, mostly exist as individual native wild species throughout the world.

With it's widespread effect on ecologies, farming & cultures, the bunny rabbit or hare is common in many parts of the globe, providing food, clothing, companionship, and artistic inspiration.

In some places, particularly Australia, New Zealand and Hawaii, introduced invasive rabbits have become a real problem, causing wide spread devastation of native species of flora and fauna. It is very important that domesticated pet rabbits never be released into the wild.

The term rabbit once referred only to the young animals but is now a general term just as another term for a young rabbit is bunny; this term is also now applied informally to all rabbits, especially domestic ones. An older term for an adult rabbit is coney; derived from the Latin cuniculus. More recently, the term kit or kitten has been used to refer to a young rabbit.

Male rabbits are called bucks, females are called does. A group of rabbits is known as a colony, nest, or occasionally a warren, though warren more commonly refers to where the rabbits live. A group of hares is called a drove and a baby hare is often called a leveret. A group of baby rabbits or leverets produced from a single mating is referred to as a litter, and a group of domestic rabbits living together is sometimes called a herd.

Rabbits and hares are herbivores that feed by grazing on grass, flowering plants, leafy weeds and tender roots. They are crepuscular, meaning they graze heavily and rapidly for roughly the first half-hour of a grazing period, usually in the late afternoon and early evening and their rhythms shift with the seasons & food supplies.

Their diets contain large amounts of plant cellulose, which is hard to digest. Rabbits and hares overcome this problem through hindgut fermentation and double ingestion. Symbiotic bacteria in their digestive system helps to digest the non-fibrous particles into a more metabolically accessible substance that is then passed as a dropping. They re-ingest their own first cycle soft droppings, which are not actually waste, in order to extract the optimum nutrition from plant substances.

 Because of the two part digestion cycle rabbits and hares pass two distinct types of droppings: soft black viscous pellets (first cycle) and hard droppings (final waste). The first cycle droppings are known as caecotrophs or night droppings and are immediately eaten, a behavior called coprophagy. The final hard pellet droppings are waste made up of indigestible straw-like fragments of plant cuticle. Hard pellets are not re-ingested.

Domesticated pet rabbits can be house trained. They can bond with humans, learn to follow simple commands and come when called. They are curious, playful, and affectionate. Their personalities vary just as with other types of pets; each bunny is different.

Rabbits DO NOT make good pets for small children; bunnies can be skittish, and shy, they are fragile and easily injured by rough handling.

They have very sharp hind claws and can bite and scratch when stressed; and are easily frightened by loud noises and sudden motions. Children should always be supervised around rabbits. Bunnies should never be held on their backs with their bellies facing up, this causes the rabbit great stress & can lead to shock, which can be deadly in some cases. A rabbit should also not have an immersive bath unless a veterinarian deems that it is necessary, as this can also lead to shock. In general bunnies are very clean & do not need bathing. To learn more about proper bunny care ask your vet or visit educational websites like: www.rabbit.org , www.rabbits.life , www.simplyrabbits.com or www.lionheadrabbitcare.com .

Owning an indoor bunny requires rabbit-proofed spaces because of their deep-seated instinctual need to chew, which is related to the fact that their teeth are always growing. Chewing household items can harm the rabbit and damage your property. Because of this, ample fresh hay for constant nibbling and pet safe chew toys should be supplied. Chew toys that are not specifically made for pets should be avoided due to the possible presence of pesticides, infectious bacteria, ticks or mites; consult your veterinarian for more information on this. Some house-rabbits are particularly fond of chewing electrical cords; they seem to find this urge irresistible, which can be very dangerous to everyone involved.

Unlike rodents bunnies & hares have two pairs of incisors in the upper jaw, the second pair, are called peg teeth and are much smaller than the front pair, they are positioned behind the longer front incisors. Rabbit teeth are open-rooted and continue to grow throughout their lives. If the animal does enough natural chewing to wear the teeth down, they will not need dental attention, but more often than not, domestic rabbits need veterinary dental care. In some rabbits, the teeth are not properly aligned, a condition called malocclusion. Because of the misaligned nature of the teeth, there is no normal wear to control the length to which the teeth grow. This condition can be very painful and result in difficulty eating and serious health problems. Malocclusion and over grown teeth should be treated by a veterinarian.

While they enjoy the security of a small nesting space they also require exercise and should be released from small hutches regularly and allowed space to run around. Bunnies need proper exercise and attention from their owners and frequently cleaned living space. In order to have a happy, healthy, well socialized bunny, you must understand the animal's needs and be able to provide for them. Becoming an educated well informed rabbit owner is very important.

Habitat & Range

Rabbit and hare habitats include meadows, woods, forests, grasslands, deserts, wetlands and as civilization encroaches their natural habitats, they are more frequently found in urban green belts as well. Rabbits live in groups, and the most widely known species, the European rabbit, live in burrows. A group of burrows is called a warren. Hares on the other hand tend to be more solitary and have above ground nests.

Rabbits and hares are prolific breeders. Thus we are reminded again that introduced rabbits have become a devastating invasive species, significantly disputing the native ecosystems for decades.

More than half the world's rabbit population resides in North America. Rabbits are also native to southwestern Europe, Southeast Asia, Sumatra, some isles of Japan, and in parts of Africa and South America. They are not naturally found in most of Eurasia, where a number of native species of hares are present. Rabbits first entered South America relatively recently. Much of the South American continent has just one species of native rabbit, the Tapeti, while most southern areas are without native rabbits.

Differences Between Rabbits and Hares

The most outstanding difference between rabbits and hares is that hares are precocial while rabbits are altricial; meaning hares are born relatively mature and mobile with hair and good vision, while rabbits are born hairless & blind, requiring more secure shelter and intensive parental care.

Hares are classified in the same family as rabbits. Hares and jackrabbits are Leporids; belonging to the genus Lepus; they are similar to rabbits in size & form and have similar but not identical herbivorous diets.

Hares tend to eat more tender bark and roots than rabbits, they generally have longer ears and live alone or in pairs. Rabbits are characterized by shorter ears fuller bodies, while hares are larger and appear to be leaner and more lanky than rabbits, with hind legs and feet that are larger and longer. Rabbits are more likely to hide from predators while hares are more likely to run. Hares are swift animals and can run up to 80 km/h (50 mph) over short distances and over longer distances, the European hare) can run up to 56 km/h (35 mph).

Normally a shy animal, the European brown hare changes its behavior in spring, when it can be seen in mid-day chasing other hares. This appears to be competition between males to attain dominance for breeding. During this spring frenzy, animals of both sexes can be seen "boxing".

Common names of these animals can leave one very confused as to which is a rabbit and which is a hare? This is because there are five Leporid species with hare in their common names but they are not scientifically considered true hares and vise versa. For example; jack-rabbits are not rabbits but are in fact hares and the domestic animal known as the Belgian hare is in fact a rabbit that was bred for meat though it does resemble a hare.

Hares and cottontail rabbits live relatively solitary lives in a simple nest above the ground, while most true rabbits live in social groups in underground burrows or warrens. Both hares and rabbits utilize speed and agility as a main defense against predators.

Rabbits use their strong claws for digging deep burrows, while hares use digging mostly to access tender edible roots and tubers or to create a depression in the ground in which to rest. Both use their claws and strong hind legs for defense along with their teeth. Each front foot has four toes plus a dewclaw. Each hind foot has four toes, but no dewclaw.

Most native wild rabbits, especially when compared to hares, have relatively full egg-shaped bodies and are smaller than domesticated breeds. Native wild rabbits and hares are generally found to have agouti coats that blend into nature, while wild introduced rabbits may have a less camouflaged appearance.

Rabbits & hares have two more upper-incisors than rodents and their tooth enamel lacks the orange tint seen in rodents.

The tails of rabbits and hares, with the exception of the cottontail species, are commonly dark on top and lighter below. Cottontails have white on the top and underside of their tails.

As a result of the position of the eyes in the skull, they both have a field of vision that encompasses nearly 360 degrees, with just a small blind spot at the bridge of the nose, this assists them in surviving predation.

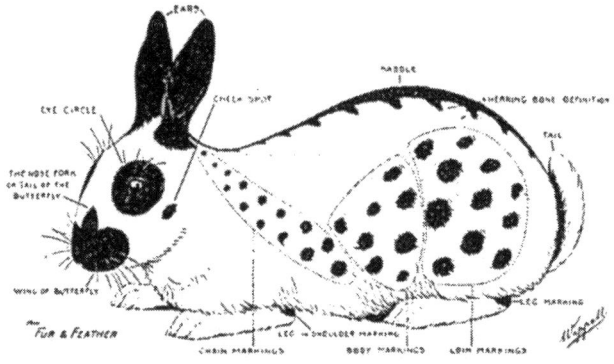

IDEAL ENGLISH RABBIT (Fur and Feather)

STANDARD OF POINTS

Head Markings

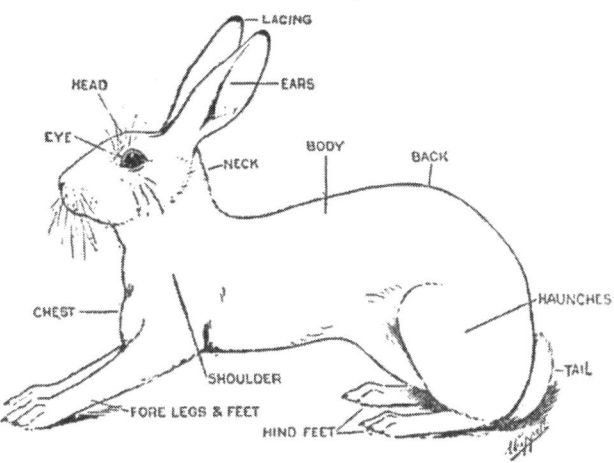

IDEAL BELGIAN HARE TYPE.
SHOWING THE REQUIRED SHAPE AND STYLE

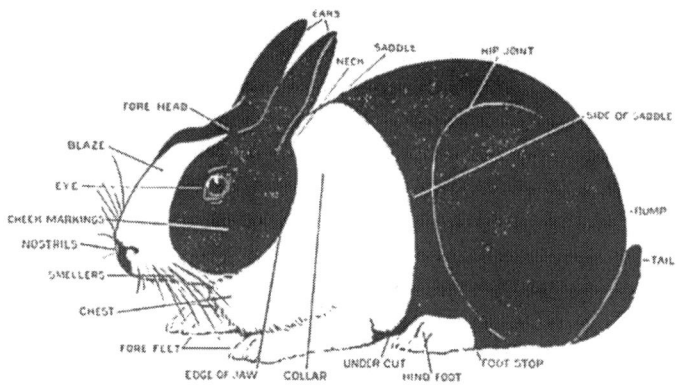

IDEAL DUTCH MARKED RABBIT (Fur and Feather)

Domestication of Rabbits

Hares have not been domesticated, rabbits on the other hand, have long been bred as livestock and kept as pets.

Beginning in the Middle Ages, the European rabbit has been widely kept as livestock, starting in ancient Rome. Selective breeding has generated a wide variety of rabbit breeds, many of which have been kept as pets since the early 19th century.

The earliest breeds were important sources of meat and through selective breeding, domesticated rabbits became larger than wild rabbits, some are also bread for specialized pelts. Though less popular than in past centuries, rabbit fur is still prized for its softness and warmth, and can be found in a broad range of colors and patterns.

The Angora rabbit breed was developed especially for its long, silky wool, which is often hand spun into yarn. Other domestic rabbit breeds have been developed primarily for the commercial fur trade, including the Rex, which has a short plush coat and is also now a popular pet.

During the Middle Ages, wild rabbits were often kept for the hunt. Monks in southern France were cross breeding rabbits at least as early as the 12th century AD.

In the 19th century, as animal fancy in general began to emerge, rabbit fanciers began to sponsor rabbit exhibitions and fairs in Western Europe and the United States. Breeds of various domesticated animals were created and modified for the added purpose of exhibition, a departure from the breeds that had been created solely for food, fur, or wool. The rabbit's emergence as a household pet began during the Victorian era.

In modern times domestic rabbit breeds come in all sizes from dwarf to giant with a variety of pets and ear shapes.

Domestic pet bunnies need proper exercise and attention from their owners and frequently cleaned living space. They must have regular checkups with a veterinarian. They need immunizations and often require dental maintenance as their teeth can grow spurs or become too long.

With the right owner education and investment of time and attention, rabbits can be trained to use a litter box, live indoors and have happy lives as pets.

Folklore

The Easter Bunny

The Easter Bunny (also called the Easter Rabbit or Easter Hare) is a folkloric figure and symbol of springtime renewal. Easter Sunday egg hunts are commonly celebrated in modern times, the Easter Bunny is depicted as a rabbit or hare bringing Easter eggs and other gifts to families. With deep roots in pagan folk traditions, the rabbit or hare as a symbol of fertility and springtime is celebrated as one of the cornerstone traditions of our modern holidays. In legend, the Easter Bunny carries colored eggs, candy, and gifts to children in a magic basket. Often these items are hidden and children take great delight in hunting for them on Easter morning.

This custom is mentioned as early as 1682 in Georg Franck von Franckenau's De ovis paschalibus ("About Easter Eggs"), referring to a German tradition of an Easter Hare bringing eggs for the children.

Eggs and bunnies have been used as fertility symbols since antiquity. The Ukrainian art of decorating eggs for Easter, known as pysanky, dates to ancient pre-Christian times.

Eggs became a symbol in Christianity associated with rebirth as early as the 1st century AD, via the iconography of the Phoenix egg, and they became associated with Easter, specifically in medieval Europe.

The Jackalope

While rabbits that appear to have horns do exist, they are not cryptids, they are actually normal animals that are suffering from an infection of cottontail papillomavirus, also known as Shope papilloma virus (SPV). This infection causes horny tumors to grow on or near the animal's head, but not always in the area where one might expect antlers. Sometimes they protrude from the neck, mouth, or cheeks. The tumors can eventually become large enough to cause the animal considerable suffering and eventually a slow painful death.

In the 1930's, hunters in northwestern Iowa reported that the rabbits they harvested had several "horn" protrusions on many parts of their bodies; including their faces and necks. SPV is a probable source of myths about the jackalope, a rabbit with the horns of an antelope, and related cryptids such as the wolpertinger, a rabbit or hare like creature of Bavarian folklore, often depicted with pheasant wings and antlers.

Stories and illustrations of horned rabbits appear in scientific treatises dating back many years, such as the Tableau encyclopédique et méthodique, from 1789 & Lepus, Hase; Lepus Cornutus; Cuniculæ porcellæ Indicæ, Kaninich, Kuniglein.Joannes, Publisher: Francofurti ad Moenum 1655

Egyptian Deities

The Hare Goddess of creation Wenet - (Wenut, Unut) is an enigmatic figure in ancient Egyptian religion and mythology. Wenet was depicted either as a hare, or as a woman with a standard bearing a recumbent hare on her head, or as a woman with the head of a hare. Wenet's name, the hieroglyphic symbol for the Hare, was the symbol of the 15th province in Upper Egypt. She was known for the gifts of renewal, regeneration, willpower & was the guardian of the underworld. Osiris was also know to take the form of a hare and be sacrificed every spring in order to perpetuate fertile renewal of the land.

According to Plutarch, the Egyptians venerated the hare because of its swiftness and keen senses, but the hare's form was also taken by certain other deities who had associations with the Otherworld. In one of the vignettes of the Elysian Fields from the Egyptian Book of the Dead, a hare-headed god, a snake-headed god, and a bull-headed god appear sitting side by side. A hare-headed deity also guards one of the Seven Halls in the Underworld.

The name means the Opener and also the Swift One. Both the snake and the hare are known for being swift creatures and the hare symbolized the opening of the new year, fertility, and the beginning of new life.

Other Folklore

The rabbit or hare is a sacred character in many cultures and often appears in folklore as the trickster archetype, as he or she uses cunningness to outwit their enemies.

Mythology and folklore about hares & rabbits is prevalent in many cultures including: Graeco-Roman, Norse, Native American, British, Welsh, German, Russian, Egyptian and many more.

In Aztec mythology, a pantheon of four hundred rabbit Gods known as Centzon Totochtin, led by Ometochtli or Two Rabbit, represented aspects of fertility, parties, and drunkenness.

In Central Africa, the common hare (Kalulu), is described as a trickster figure.

In Chinese folklore, rabbits accompany changes of the moon. In the Chinese New Year, the rabbit is one of the twelve celestial animals in the Chinese zodiac.

In Japanese tradition, rabbits live on the moon, where they make delicious mochi, the popular snack of mashed sticky rice. This comes from interpreting the pattern of dark patches on the moon as a rabbit sitting on its tiptoes, pounding on a Japanese mortar.

In Korean mythology, as in Japanese, rabbits live on the moon making rice cakes ("Tteok" in Korean).

A Vietnamese mythological story portrays the rabbit of innocence and youthfulness. The Gods of the myth are shown to be hunting and killing rabbits to show off their power.

In Jewish folklore, rabbits (shfanim שפנים) are associated with cowardice, a usage still current in contemporary Israeli spoken Hebrew (similar to the English colloquial use of chicken to denote cowardice).

In Celtic and Irish mythology rabbits and hares are magical. They can represent the Goddess of dawn, flight, timidity, witchcraft, the ability to shapeshift, visitations from the spirits of the dead and bad luck in farming. The female Irish hare is larger than the male and they may be the oldest living Irish mammal. Currently the Irish hare, which only exists in Ireland, is at risk of becoming endangered due to conflict with modern farming.

In another Anglo-Celtic tradition, if the first words you speak upon waking on the first day of each month are "rabbit, rabbit, rabbit" you will invoke good luck. According to old folk lore the words should be spoken up the chimney to be most effective. The word rabbit was often used in expletives, and suggests that this folk-charm may have origins the ancient belief that swearing could be used as a means of warding against evil.

In Anishinaabe traditional beliefs, held by the Ojibwe and some other Native American peoples, Nanabozho, or Great Rabbit, is an important deity related to the creation of the world.

The rabbit as a trickster is still a part of American pop culture today. Anthropomorphized rabbits have appeared in film and literature over the decades, including but limited to: Br'er Rabbit from African-American folktales, Bugs Bunny from Warner Brothers, The Tortoise & the Hare, the White Rabbit and the March Hare from Alice's Adventures in Wonderland, and the Peter Rabbit and Benjamin Bunny stories by Beatrix Potter.

Buddhism, Christianity, and Judaism have associations with an ancient circular motif called the three rabbits (or three hares). Its meaning ranges from peace and tranquility, to purity, or the Holy Trinity, to Kabbalistic levels of the soul or to the Jewish diaspora. The tripartite symbol also appears in heraldry and in modern culture.

In 2004 an interesting research project was launched tracing the origins and migration of the symbolic images using three hares with conjoined ears.

In this image, three hares are seen chasing each other in a circle with their heads near its center. While each of the animals appears to have two ears, only three ears are depicted. The ears form a triangle at the center of the circle and each is shared by two of the hares.

The image has been traced from Christian churches in the English county of Devon, back along the Silk Road to China, through western and eastern Europe and the Middle East.

It was possibly first depicted in the Middle East and then in China, before being reimported into other cultures centuries later. Its use is associated with Christian, Jewish, Islamic and Buddhist sites possibly stretching back as far as 600 CE.

The folklore and mythology old and new regarding hares and rabbits is so abundant that a complete discussion could not possibly be included here.

Please Note: This book talks about common rabbit behaviors as they relate to observation being used as a tool for understanding your bunny's needs & expressions.

It is NOT a rabbit care guide.

Taking good care of your bunny in very important , every rabbit owner should educate themselves on the details of proper rabbit care and ask their veterinarian for referrals to proper cares guides.

Bunny Talk

Field Notes

Human and Animal Communication

There are some behaviors that humans and other species have in common and this fact fosters a natural avenue of interspecies communication based on instinctual reactions.

One scientific study has found that humans, 30 bird species and 29 species of mammals share the same pattern of pitch and speed in their basic messages.

Humans and these 59 species are intrinsically able to understand each other when it comes to: aggression, hostility, appeasement, approachability, submission and fear. [01]

In general human and animal communication is not unusual or extraordinary, it can be observed in everyday life wherever there are humans and animals living together.

The interactions between pets and their owners, or farm animals and their keepers for example, reflect this interspecies dialogue. As owners & animals learn to discern the other's behavior the dialog can become a detailed two-way communication.

What is extraordinary is the level to which the depth of this communication can be taken when humans dedicate themselves to connecting with & understanding individual animals.

Much of the human component of gaining an accurate understanding what an animal is expressing depends on gaining knowledge of what is normal for that species and for that individual animal, as well as what constitutes unusual behavior.

It is also important to take into account that in spite of our common instinctual expressions, non-human species communicate differently than we do & may interpret the signals from humans differently than humans themselves.

The interpretive baseline for interactions is always based in the foundational communication methods of that species and not based on human communication standards. For example, apes, horses & parrots are capable of complex communications with humans but their baselines for friendly behavior have definite differences.

Successful interspecies communication requires correct interpretation of complex and sometimes subtle cues from both parties.

Skillful interpretation of animal communication and behavior may be critical to the welfare of animals and owners alike. It's important to learn to recognize behaviors that indicate, stress, pain or panic in an animal.

Just as with human-to-human communication, there will be misunderstandings but with effort, research and education humans can become better and better at understanding their animal companions.

When a human is attempting to have pleasant interactions with a new animal there are several things that support success:

- Be calm and think only kind thoughts, if you are agitated the animal will instinctually pick up on it.

- Avoid strong perfumes, deodorants, soaps & lotions, these are often way too strong for sensitive animal noses.

- Move slowly, stay where the animal can see you & keep your voice steady & soft but firm.

- Allow the animal time to get used to your presence & your scent.

- If the animal does not want you to touch it, refrain from reaching out to pet it, be satisfied just to be in its vicinity & let it learn you are not a threat. Be patient, over time the animal may initiate contact with you when it is sure you are safe to inter act with.

With effort, education & patience many people can learn the intricacies of better communication with animals different types.

You can learn more about interacting with all types of animals at:

https://www.youtube.com/c/animalwondersmontana

Basic Rabbit Communication

Rabbit language is unique and each individual bunny will have its own quirks involving ears, tail, nose, sounds, body position and behavior. Understanding bunny communication takes education and attentive observation.

The following is a very basic list of common bunny behaviors & **possible meanings**, if you own a bunny I encourage you to do some in-depth research on the subject to discover standard rabbit behavior and the special nuances of your bunny's communication.

(There are blank boxes provided for you to add your own observations.)

Perking :
Body slightly tense, looking in a particular direction, ears perked up and slightly forward., nose twitching as they analyze the smells, may include standing on back legs to get a better view .-- This means your bunny is assessing a noise or movement or scent and is prepared to run if they sense danger.

Stress Tooth Grinding or Chattering & Whimper Grunts:
The rabbit is loudly grinding its teeth or it is making a distressed grunting whimpering noise. -- Indicates unhappiness, stress, fear and may indicate illness or pain. Ask your vet about what you should do.

Tooth Purring:
The rabbit is grinding its teeth gently (may be accompanied by gentle oinking or huffing noises) -- This means your bunny is relaxed, happy & content.

Chewing on Metal Bars of the Cage:
The bunny is chewing & prying on the cage with it's teeth. -- This can simply mean your bunny needs to get out of the cage & get some exercise or maybe it needs more chew toys but it can also be a stress behavior or related to poor diet or dental issues. You should find a way to prevent this behavior as it can cause or worsen dental problems. Contact your vet for advice.

Boxing Posture:
The rabbits sitting up, ears usually perked, standing on their hind legs (standing their ground) with forepaws raised ready to swat or punch, they may also make a growling noise. -- This can mean your bunny is afraid or upset but is taking a stand, it feels threatened and perhaps territorial.

Hunching with Ears Back &/or Belly Pressing:
A bunny in a tense hunched loaf-like position or pressing their belly to the floor or holding their belly up off of the floor, with their ears back with unusual breathing & facial squinting or whimpering sounds.– Rabbits have delicate digestive systems. This is usually a sign of an unwell bunny, both belly positions can indicate illness or digestive problems. Belly pressing on a cool surface may also mean your bunny is overheated & needs to be moved to a cooler place with drinking water available. Regardless of cause, this is usually a sign of distress, it could be a serious issue you should talk to your vet about it.

Thumping:
Your rabbit thumps their hind legs loudly against the ground. -- Sometimes thumping is used as an alarm to tell everyone that danger is near. It can also be a warning that says "Get away from me!!" Thumping & serious aggressive lunging means your bunny is mad or annoyed, feels like they are in danger or displeased because they feel their territory or belongings are being violated. Some sassy bunnies thump in protest to being told "no".

Lunging & Head Butting:
The animal charges forward as if to drive you away. -- Lunging or head butting can be both a playful aggression & a serious attack.
Just like cats & dogs, a rabbit can show playful aggression but they can also lunge or butt as a form of aggressive self defense that tells you your bunny is mad or annoyed. You will just need to pay attention so you can tell the difference between the two.

The Relaxed Loaf Position:
The loaf position is when your rabbit is sprawled out on the floor and looks like a loaf of bread. -- This is a sign of relaxation and comfort. It means that they want to be left in peace and they are feeling secure, peaceful and maybe ready to take a nice nap.

Screaming & Squealing:
The rabbit makes a loud shrill noise & may be trembling or making an extreme effort to flee or take cover.-- This is a sign of extreme distress, it means the rabbit is very frightened or in a lot of pain or both. You should try to figure out the cause & eliminate it, you may need to contact your vet if this was not a reaction to being spooked or if your bunny is injured. Placing your bunny in a cool dark quiet place may help them calm down.

Turning Their Back to You:
The animal turns its butt to you & refuses to face you or engage with you.-- This means "Leave me alone, I have had enough". You will see this in some bunnies when they are mad, stressed or overstimulated. Leave them in peace for a while & then check back after they have had a break.

Chin Rub Scent Marking:
The rabbit will rub their chin against furniture, door frames, or anywhere they want to leave a scent mark; it says "I am here & this is mine" -- Rabbits have scent glands under their chins and they rub their scent marking on items to claim them or mark their territory in general. If your bunny chins you it is claiming you as a member of their colony.

Playful Head Butting, Bumps, Nudges:
The rabbit nudges & bumps you while exhibiting happy behaviors like zooming, oinking & binkies.-- This means "Play with me or pay attention to me."

The Binky Jump Twist & Zooming in Circle :
A high jump and body twist in the air or a more subtle low jump & twist with bursts of energy, running or "zooming" around the room. You should be careful not to trip over them. (may include oinking noises) – This is the bunny equivalent of a dog wagging their tail or a cat purring & rubbing your legs, it means your rabbit is excited and happy. If your bunny zooms in circles around your feet it is a sign of affection. Be careful not to step on them.

Scattering Poops:
The bunny is leaving droppings all around an area. -- This is one way that a bunny claims their territory. It is usually a temporary behavior but each bunny is different, some bunnies like to reinforce their claim by repeating this behavior.

Pushing or Tossing Objects Around:
The bunny is picking up small objects in its mouth & flipping them in the air or pushing them around with their nose. -- This is how many bunnies play. They enjoy toys that they can butt, nose & toss. It might be a good time to get new toys.

The Cautious Slow Tip-toe :
The bunny is doing a slow tip-toe with their ears forward and their tails down, pausing often to look around.-- This means your bunny is not sure about people, objects or the space around them. It is a common behavior in situations that are new. Just give your bunny time to get used to things.

Aggressive Bumps, Nudges and Nips:
Your bunny butts you somewhat aggressively with its head & may bite you gently. -- The bunny wants you to give it space or move out of its way, sometimes this is a reaction to dislike of strong smells like perfume, soap or hand lotion.

Honking & Oinking:
The bunny makes a grunting noise, like oinking or honking, often while excited or running around. -- This is usually a happy noise, your bunny is excited & pleased but there is also a type of honking that is part of mating behavior.

Not Eating or Not Pooping: Your rabbit stops eating in their regular pattern &/or is not regularly passing poops.
If your bunny stops eating or pooping it is important to contact your vet.
If a bunny stops eating for even one day it can be life threatening. Even skipping one meal can indicate a serious issue developing. Take a moment to investigate their food & water source, make sure its clean & fresh. Not pooping also indicates a serious problem. Make a note of changes in recent droppings. Contact your vet right away for advice.

Flopping:
The animal is flopped on its side, is very still & is resting, sometimes they even roll all the way onto their back. It almost looks like the rabbit is dead -- Don't panic. If your rabbits breathing is regular & relaxed & they are responsive, this is a sign that the rabbit feels completely safe & relaxed. A rabbit flop can actually look a little scary for new rabbit owners but if you look closely, you'll see your rabbit is fine, they are just very relaxed & contently resting.

Spraying Urine:
Male and female bunnies will spray urine. -- They are marking their territory & communication their readiness to mate. Un-neutered males will even mark female rabbits and their territory by spraying them with urine. Un-spayed females may also exabit this behavior. It's one more good reason to spay or neuter your rabbits.

Itching & Scratching:
Your bunny seems to be scratching a lot -- Excessive itching & scratching is not normal, you need to figure out why this is happening. There are many causes, from mites & fleas, to infections & allergies. Sores, bald spots or residue in the ears indicate that there is a problem. Contact your vet for advice.

Mouth Breathing or Drooling:
Your bunny is breathing through its mouth instead of the classic bunny nose breathing, some times you must look very closely to notice it. Or you bunny is drooling. -- This is not normal, rabbits do not naturally breath through their mouth, nor do they drool like dogs, it is a sign that something is not right. Contact your vet for advice.

Puffy Belly:
Your bunny's belly looks bloated; rounder & puffier than normal. -- This can be a sign of a serious problem, especially if its firm to the touch. Contact your vet right away for instructions.

Dirty Bunny:
Your bunny is not keeping itself clean, its fur may appear greasy or matted or it may have a dirty butt. -- Rabbits are naturally very clean & groom themselves well. Lack of grooming may indicate that your bunny is not feeling well or that it needs a little help with grooming. Also check to see if their enclosure needs more frequent cleaning.

Grumpy Bunny:
Your bunny is unusually irritable & not its usual friendly self. -- This can happen in pubescent bunnies as mating hormones start raging, but it can also be a sign that some thing is wrong, look for signs of illness, injury or stress. If your rabbit seems unpleased with something try to eliminate it if possible. Getting your rabbit fixed usually puts an end to irritability caused by mating hormones.

Head Tilt:
The bunny is tilting its head to one side and unable to put its head in a normal position. They may be clumsy & unable to eat or move normally, their eyes may move in a spastic manner.-- **CALL YOUR VET RIGHT AWAY.** Head tilt indicates a neurological condition. There are several possible causes & early treatment is important to your rabbits survival. Head tilt can be deadly or become a permeant condition.

Mounting:
The bunny climbs onto the back of another rabbit.-- In addition to being a sexual mating behavior, mounting is a dominance behavior. Rabbits will try to claim their dominance over others in the group this way. If you have more than one rabbit you are likely to see some mounting behavior. This will happen even if you have rabbits of the same gender & they have been fixed.

Trancing & Shock:
The bunny become immobile & may look as though they are playing dead with legs in a stiff locked position or they may go completely limp & unresponsive.-- This is called **Tonic Immobility**, it is a fearful stress reaction. Frozen trance state is a crisis state where the bunny's heart is racing & can be a very serious danger. If your bunny does not recover very quickly from trancing you should consider it an emergency. **CONTACT YOUR VET RIGHT AWAY**. Even if your bunny recovers quickly you should still call your vet for instructions.

Sometimes people think Trancing is just a harmless behavior & may use it to complete grooming tasks, but it is in fact a dangerous fearful stress reaction & can lead to shock.
Shock is a cascading effect where in the animals organs are under so much stress they begin to shut down. Many rabbits can recover from shock if given proper care. Be sure to ask you vet how to recognize & deal with trancing & shock in your bunny.

Learn more about Rabbits At:
www.youtube.com/c/animalwondersmontana , just search this channel for Rabbits.
You can find an A to Z List of Rabbit Behavior at:
www.bunnyhugga.com/a-to-z/rabbit-behaviour

My Bunny Behavior & Communication Log:

Behaviors, Dates, Meanings, Comments

Bunny Notes:

Bunny Notes:

Bunny Notes:

Bunny Notes:

Bunny Notes:

Bunny Notes:

Bunny Notes:

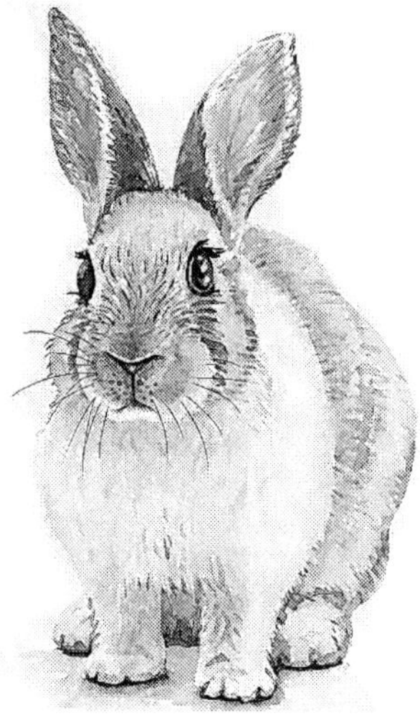

Bunny Notes:

Bunny Notes:

Bunny Poems

Dark gray is his color,
 Brown are his eyes.
His ears appear reaching
 Up toward the skies.

In the moonlight, on a bright night,
    Wee folk, wild folk, gather.
Frisky and gay, Cottontails they,
    To the garden scamper.

Four furry little legs—just four—
These are the hind, these are the fore;
These do the digging, hands are they;
These do the jumping night and day.

Oh, who has seen my bunny?
  For he has strayed away;
Will some one help me find
    him,
  And bring him home to stay?

I wonder what's the meaning
  Of these tracks in the
    snow—
The tiny tracks so winding,
  That seem nowhere to go!

Across the snow last ev'ning
  I think he hopped away!
Ah, there you are, my
    bunny—
  My bunny rabbit gray!

Reference Calendar

If the first words you speak upon waking on the first day of each month are "rabbit, rabbit, rabbit" you will invoke good luck.

2022

January
M	T	W	T	F	S	S
					1	2
3	4	5	6	7	8	9
10	11	12	13	14	15	16
17	18	19	20	21	22	23
24	25	26	27	28	29	30
31						

February
M	T	W	T	F	S	S
	1	2	3	4	5	6
7	8	9	10	11	12	13
14	15	16	17	18	19	20
21	22	23	24	25	26	27
28						

March
M	T	W	T	F	S	S
	1	2	3	4	5	6
7	8	9	10	11	12	13
14	15	16	17	18	19	20
21	22	23	24	25	26	27
28	29	30	31			

April
M	T	W	T	F	S	S
				1	2	3
4	5	6	7	8	9	10
11	12	13	14	15	16	17
18	19	20	21	22	23	24
25	26	27	28	29	30	

May
M	T	W	T	F	S	S
						1
2	3	4	5	6	7	8
9	10	11	12	13	14	15
16	17	18	19	20	21	22
23	24	25	26	27	28	29
30	31					

June
M	T	W	T	F	S	S
		1	2	3	4	5
6	7	8	9	10	11	12
13	14	15	16	17	18	19
20	21	22	23	24	25	26
27	28	29	30			

July
M	T	W	T	F	S	S
				1	2	3
4	5	6	7	8	9	10
11	12	13	14	15	16	17
18	19	20	21	22	23	24
25	26	27	28	29	30	31

August
M	T	W	T	F	S	S
1	2	3	4	5	6	7
8	9	10	11	12	13	14
15	16	17	18	19	20	21
22	23	24	25	26	27	28
29	30	31				

September
M	T	W	T	F	S	S
			1	2	3	4
5	6	7	8	9	10	11
12	13	14	15	16	17	18
19	20	21	22	23	24	25
26	27	28	29	30		

October
M	T	W	T	F	S	S
					1	2
3	4	5	6	7	8	9
10	11	12	13	14	15	16
17	18	19	20	21	22	23
24	25	26	27	28	29	30
31						

November
M	T	W	T	F	S	S
	1	2	3	4	5	6
7	8	9	10	11	12	13
14	15	16	17	18	19	20
21	22	23	24	25	26	27
28	29	30				

December
M	T	W	T	F	S	S
			1	2	3	4
5	6	7	8	9	10	11
12	13	14	15	16	17	18
19	20	21	22	23	24	25
26	27	28	29	30	31	

2023

January
M	T	W	T	F	S	S
						1
2	3	4	5	6	7	8
9	10	11	12	13	14	15
16	17	18	19	20	21	22
23	24	25	26	27	28	29
30	31					

February
M	T	W	T	F	S	S
		1	2	3	4	5
6	7	8	9	10	11	12
13	14	15	16	17	18	19
20	21	22	23	24	25	26
27	28					

March
M	T	W	T	F	S	S
		1	2	3	4	5
6	7	8	9	10	11	12
13	14	15	16	17	18	19
20	21	22	23	24	25	26
27	28	29	30	31		

April
M	T	W	T	F	S	S
					1	2
3	4	5	6	7	8	9
10	11	12	13	14	15	16
17	18	19	20	21	22	23
24	25	26	27	28	29	30

May
M	T	W	T	F	S	S
1	2	3	4	5	6	7
8	9	10	11	12	13	14
15	16	17	18	19	20	21
22	23	24	25	26	27	28
29	30	31				

June
M	T	W	T	F	S	S
			1	2	3	4
5	6	7	8	9	10	11
12	13	14	15	16	17	18
19	20	21	22	23	24	25
26	27	28	29	30		

July
M	T	W	T	F	S	S
					1	2
3	4	5	6	7	8	9
10	11	12	13	14	15	16
17	18	19	20	21	22	23
24	25	26	27	28	29	30
31						

August
M	T	W	T	F	S	S
	1	2	3	4	5	6
7	8	9	10	11	12	13
14	15	16	17	18	19	20
21	22	23	24	25	26	27
28	29	30	31			

September
M	T	W	T	F	S	S
				1	2	3
4	5	6	7	8	9	10
11	12	13	14	15	16	17
18	19	20	21	22	23	24
25	26	27	28	29	30	

October
M	T	W	T	F	S	S
						1
2	3	4	5	6	7	8
9	10	11	12	13	14	15
16	17	18	19	20	21	22
23	24	25	26	27	28	29
30	31					

November
M	T	W	T	F	S	S
		1	2	3	4	5
6	7	8	9	10	11	12
13	14	15	16	17	18	19
20	21	22	23	24	25	26
27	28	29	30			

December
M	T	W	T	F	S	S
				1	2	3
4	5	6	7	8	9	10
11	12	13	14	15	16	17
18	19	20	21	22	23	24
25	26	27	28	29	30	31

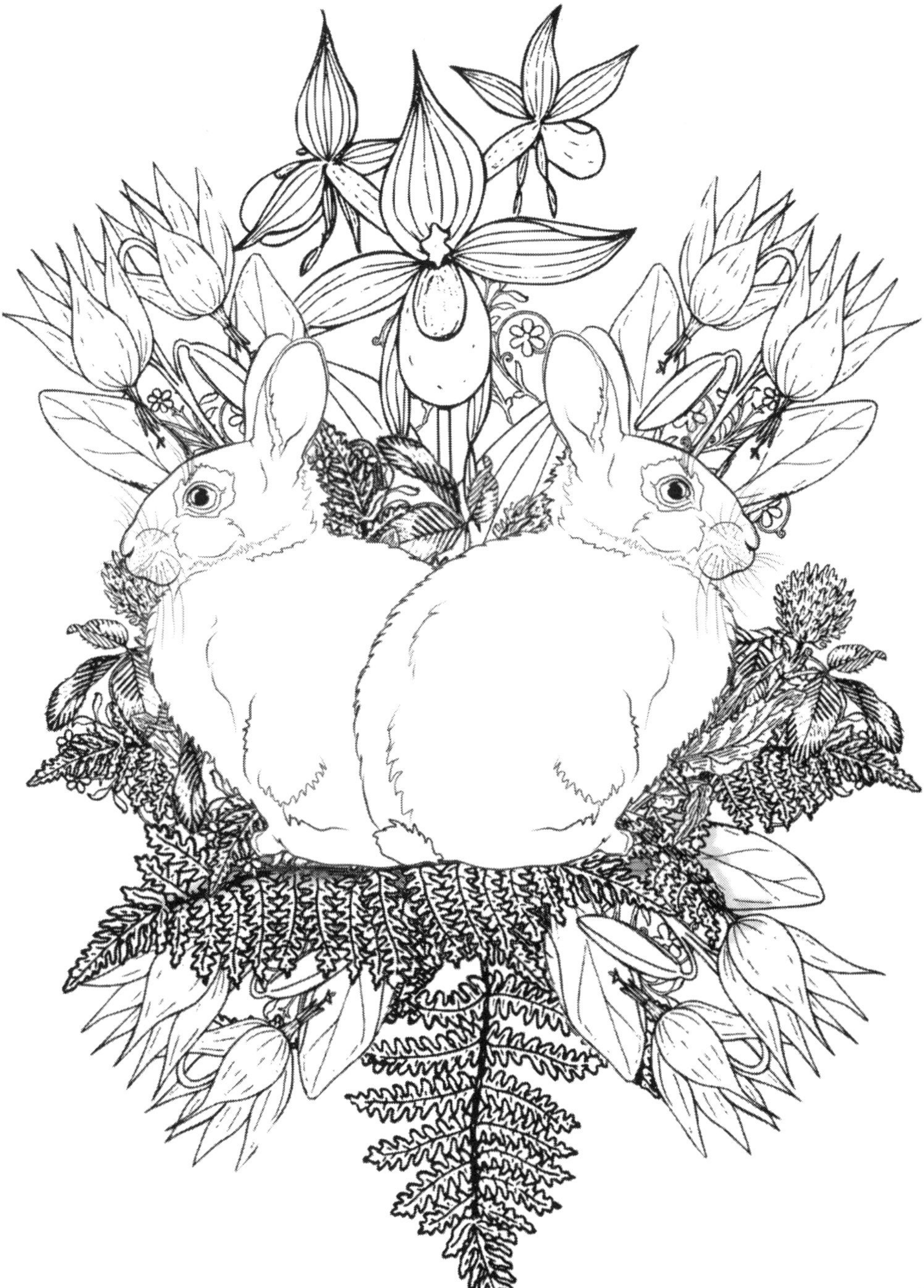

THE END

Compiled, Written & Created
by Dianne Keast
Perfectly Sane Publishing
Journals & Books by Request
Copyright 2021

Sources

SOURCES

About Bunny Rabbits & Hares Research sources:
Foundational Information:
wikipedia.org,
deities.fandom.com/wiki
en.wikipedia.org/wiki/Rabbit_rabbit_rabbit
en.wikipedia.org/wiki/Animal_communication
en.wikipedia.org/wiki/Human%E2%80%93animal_communication
en.wikipedia.org/wiki/Animal_language
en.wikipedia.org/wiki/Animal_communication

Deities Associated With Hares and Rabbits
https://mythsymbolsandplay.typepad.com/my-blog/2017/03/deities-associated-with-hares-and-rabbits.html

[01]: **Animal talk: breaking the codes of animal language** by Friend, Tim, Publication date 2004
https://archive.org/details/animaltalk00timf/page/90/mode/2up

Michabo The Great Hare
mythsymbolsandplay.typepad.com
https://iseumsanctuary.com/2018/03/31/the-hare-goddess-wenet/
iseumsanctuary.com/2020/04/05/the-hare-goddess-wenet-part

Other Research Sources:
www.bunnylady.com
www.rabbit.org
www.petsial.com
www.language.rabbitspeak.com
www.rabbits.life
www.simplyrabbits.com
www.terriwindling.com/blog/2014/12/thefolklore-of-rabbits-hares.html
www.lionheadrabbitcare.com/belgian-hare
www.lionheadrabbitcare.com/rabbit-vs-hare-differences
www.bunnyhugga.com/a-to-z/rabbit-behaviour
www.en.wikipedia.org/wiki/Hare
www.mohrs.org/rabbit-teeth-how-they-work
www.youtube.com/c/animalwondersmontana

Image:
Three Hares — Coat Of Arms
Blason ville fr Corbenay (Haute-Saône)
Wikimedia Commons, the free media repository
www.commons.wikimedia.org/wiki/File:Blason_ville_fr_Corbenay_(Haute-Sa%C3%B4ne).svg#filelinks

Public Domain Poem Sources:

Nixie Bunny in Manners-land, by Sindelar,
Joseph Charles, Illustrated by **Geraldine Hodge, Helen.**
1885- [from old catalog],
Chicago, Beckley-Cardy company [1912],
Call Number/Physical Location- PZ7.S615 Ni,
Digital Id http://hdl.loc.gov/loc.gdc/scd0001.00020765033,, dcmsiabooks.nixiebunnyinmann00sind,
Library of Congress Control Number 12023067
public domain and are free to use and reuse

More Public Domain Image Sources:

The American pet stock standard of perfection and official guide to the American fur fanciers' association by American fur fancier's association, Wagner, J. Henri, 1881- 1915, Public Domain- The Library of Congress, Identifier-ark:/13960/t9086xk7g (appears interior & on vintage style back cover)

Our Fancy Rabbits from Engraved images from the Boy's own Paper, 1880- 1890 digitized by seriykotik1970 is marked as CC PDM 1.0 www.flickr.com/photos/71092566@N00/46399223554 (appears on vintage style front cover)

Fighting Hares Object number rRP-T-2015-41-1544, Henri Verstijnen1892 – 1940 Public Domain, www.hdl.handle.net/10934/RM0001.COLLECT.627209, www.rijksmuseum.nl

Lepus, Hase; Lepus Cornutus; Cuniculæ porcellæ Indicæ, Kaninich, Kuniglein.Joannes, 1603- 1675, Publisher: Francofurti ad Moenum 1655 -Identifier (UUID): ea34fa80-c6d0-012f-2e54- 58d385a7bc34, Public Domain, New Your Public Library www.digitalcollections.nypl.orgJonstonus.

Pantheon egyptien : collection des personnages mythologiques de l'ancienne Egypte, d'apres les monuments, avec un texte explicative, Dubois, L. J. J. (Leon Jean Joseph) (Artist) Champollion, Jean François (1790-1832) Date Issued: 1823 – 1825, Place: A Paris, Publisher: De L'imprimerie de Firmin Didot .Identifier (UUID): 2a832730-c6d4-012f-7fe5-58d385a7bc34, Public Domain, New Your Public Library, www.digitalcollections.nypl.org/items/510d47d9-5b7b-a3d9-e040-e00a18064a99

Rabbits – *digitized by seriykotik1970, uploaded on January 6, 2019*
Marked Public Domain
www.flickr.com/photos/seriykotik/45908761414/in/photolist-2icpaTS-2dG99D1-apyuTR-2cWNpkd

Other Public Domain digital Images used in derivative works sourced from these websites:
Wikapedia.org,
commons.wikimedia.org,
rawpixel.com/category/53/public-domain,
pixabay.com,
publicdomainvectors.org

All Cover Image Components Sourced from Pixabay.com unless otherwise noted.

Images secondary to text or other content are used under current commercial license.

Made in the USA
Columbia, SC
14 April 2024